Enough!

by

Damien B. Donnelly

First published 2022 by The Hedgehog Poetry Press

Published in the UK by
The Hedgehog Poetry Press
5, Coppack House
Churchill Avenue
Clevedon
BS21 6QW

www.hedgehogpress.co.uk

ISBN: 978-1-913499-73-0

9 8 7 6 5 4 3 2 1

A CIP Catalogue record for this book is available from the British Library.

Memory is mischievous when it twists past a door

long since shut.

Première Partie: The Leaning In

Deuxième Partie: The Living

Troisième Partie: The Loving

Quatrième Partie: The Moving

Cinquième Partie: The Leaning Out

Sixième Partie: The Leaving

Première Partie: The Leaning In

98, RUE VIEILLE DU TEMPLE

On Monday,
       a muse-filled Monday, a sky-blue clarity
carries, unlike the water in a single river, from sea
            back to source.
The pace is steady, still stepping up on that spiral,
but memory is mischievous and twists past a door
            long since shut
on a turret staircase now strained with ideals where
youth once lived and I wonder if all the sunflowers
            I painted on its walls of
other people's smoke stains are still visible under
the time that's grown over it. Considerations, here,
            today, after Van Gogh,
after all the running from the reverb of those shots
and from the call of those crows that tried too hard
            to claw at the dream
we sketched, once, beyond those walls.

TROIS COULEURS ET MOI

after the film *Trois Couleurs Bleu* staring Juliette Binoche

I was growing out of green when I first saw you in Dublin,
watching you brush bare knuckle across a cinematic screen.

You; sipping coffee in a corner café, courting violin blues
on a street not yet mine, and me; still trying to come out,

to put away childish things; trainers, retainers, dressing up
as cowboys and wondering why Indians wanted to survive,

stretching out over the vast arrays of nothingness, in chaps
someone, somewhere, once thought were suitable for a kid,

still empty, still trying to fill in bare spaces on pants, prints,
persons, noticeable for nothing; rien, comme tu m'avais dit

from that big screen in a cinema where no one ate popcorn.
You, looking for an apartment in the 5th where I later came

to sleep, shit, smoke, slip, to bash my own knuckles against
banal and back again, to seduce ideas of being a somebody

having already left everybody, even the concerning costumes
and those three colours that had started out with you, back

when I was green, though only in part, and coveting Julie;
perhaps a prophesy for the coming of the Blue. Sometimes,

the endings are there to be seen, right at the very beginning.

*In Trois Couleurs Bleu, Juliette Binoche's character Julie moves to Paris and lives in
the 5ème arrondissement where I lived when I first moved to Paris in 1997.

COLLEGE DES IRLANDAIS

Giggling into plastic cups, Bacardi breaths staining
the walls priests once beat beads against. Fresh-faced
smuggler of prohibited drinks and that unidentified
style of French *fille* testing the strength of Irish roots
on the springs of his bog-pressured bed.

Two bodies taking that final leap off youth's diving
board, forms still to be identified in their own right
away from booze, from the breath and that tiny bed
that held the weight of their unblemished bodies,
beautifully.

One room, one window, one former convent now
a curator to two kids playing at grown-up, imitating
the art their parents hung in frames over fireplaces
because their parents had mentioned it in passing.
Novices, taking notes on how it felt to hold secrets,
break rules, kiss girls and boys

                    outside of lust or longing

over a cobbled street by the Pantheon where souls
of celebrated greats all slept together, still, beyond
breath and the excuse needed of Bacardi in plastic
cups housing tastes that couldn't yet be identified.

*Le Collège des Irlandais, formerly a polish seminary, is home to CCI, Le
Centre Culturel Irlandais and has long been a residence for Irish students
abroad and I lived there for a few months at the end of 1997.

AN AUTUMN OF AMATEURS

Autumn hanging off trees, artist in the opening air,
trying to discover the right colour for a character
at the far shade of the bloom. Autumn withering

on the leaves, shivering in the shade of that Y2K
that never came to be; the fake lies, fake news,
faking findings to satisfy his ego, painting Picassos'

with colourless pencils before learning the difference
between myth and man. It can be cold on the other side
of gullible, seasons don't have the right suitcases to pack

what's required and even those cases don't come with
compartments equipped with bandages to attend to pride
after it's been found waiting, in those foreign fields. Art,

like autumn, does not come without practice, early on
it's all about the dabbles; shadow in the shade, studies of
still life, sedated on canvases on a single seat of Monday's

shade, in parks, in Paris, on a pale-faced boy still too mild
to identify fact from frame. Fast movement needed before
winter rains wiped him forgotten before begun.

5, RUE DES IRLANDAIS

Unpolished expats
crumbling croissant breakfasts at the far end of a crisp hall,
missing those milky teas and smothered bacon the mothers
would have forced down throats on rainy days in houses
far from this place not yet called home;
a convent the Polish left to the Irish,
who then left drunken trickles of cheap wine on every table
on *Mouffetard*, next to the marketeers of Place Monge where
we all tried cheese that stank like stale socks while we wore
the same socks for consecutive days
to save on laundry.
I found Hemingway here, later, who had been there earlier
and Julie too, who'd had nothing in Blue. *A Moveable Feast*
he called it. Moveable. We were too young to be celebrated
by a feast,
too new to be owners of anything
except green gills and half hopes; the hope for a little heat
and butter with breakfast, a letter in the post before it came
coldly on computers, later, without a trace of that longing
etched into lines of each individual letter
by every single mother.
All things change; like ownership, taste, timings, the things
we held on to and the others we let go of, like the concept
of a home, while forever in motion. We had nothing once,
in the cold end of a big hall
in Paris, in the 5th
by the Pantheon with all its buried heroes and the Sorbonne
with all its protestors who'd all departed by our day, having
since surrendered their brave boots, in time, for softer soles.

LADY, DON'T LOVE ME NOW

Reprised marshland, once home to Kings, since coloured over
in queens and McQueen, once pierced by the needle playing

Tin Angel, Joni singing as I flipped off Solitaire. Tossing decks
of paper-thin royals beneath painted sunflowers as the Marquis

beat herself in the bedroom, fidgeting her fevered fingers over
tarnished diamonds in the empty trenches of desire, waiting

to discard the dream, wanting courtly flatmate to climb back
inside a closet, to appease the hunger she wore on the sleeves

of her figure-hugging voluptuous virginity.

Stepping stones or sinking sand. In the corridor, worn boards
ached under footsteps raising more than rafters; blonde cubs

who came occasionally, just to tease with all their milliseconds
of naughty nothings. The distractions from twists and turns,

from strained beginnings in the moisture of all the marchland
they'd given to the sticky fingers of all those Jews, after Kings

and colourful queens and starving Joni wannabes, often idolised,
occasionally canonised or left alone, playing Solitaire in shadow.

---

*Le Marais, located in the 3ème and 4ème arrondissements, was formerly a
marshland, hence the name, which was reclaimed, first for royalty which you can
still see at Place des Vosges and later populated by the Jews who were followed by
the LGBTQ+ community who, in turn, were followed by designer shops. *Stepping
stones or sinking sand* is a line from the song 'I think I Understand' from Joni
Mitchell's album *Clouds* which I was just discovering at the time, which also
features the song *Tin Angel*.

14

62, RUE D'ALESIA

After Henry Millar and Anaïs Nin who dined, dated and desired at Le Zeyer

I used to sit here sipping cocktails I couldn't afford
just because you sat here years before me, drinking
lust from lips that weren't yours. I used to sit here

in the heady heat of all you had eaten of each other,
wondering if I stayed long enough would I be able
to taste what it was like to devour all that desire.

I used to come here, to scribble down all I might
one day forget and I wondered if she forgot you
as quickly as she turned the page to the next date

in her diary.

THREE BOYS AND A GIRL

diving from teens into twenties at the end of the nineties,
wearing hangovers like la Légion d'Honneur,

hot under summer's press and last night's sweat, still sweet.
She laughs, he blushes and we fuck

his naked imprint for days against the glass, reflections of cuts
yet to be made. Some things are only meant for the moon

like stars and darkness and emptiness and his lips.

Three boys and a girl in a summer's park, one fair, one dark
and the flippant I'd recently flipped off and over,

now stuck like sweaty patches under arms you can't avoid
looking at, sniffing, wondering how long they'll take to dry off.

Sitting, sweating, smiling, lusting it large in a perfect park,
in the heat of his sweat, her smile and those eyes

burning ourselves with the first tastes of belonging.

* *La Légion d'Honneur* is the highest order of merit in France, established in
1802 by Napoleon Bonaparte

OUT OF SEASON

Green spots where rain drops, I was burnt brown
and yellow, unfolding from late autumn
in the midst of a summer your city couldn't control

even with all your habits

and you were as much *habillé* in tradition as your streets
were dressed in concrete. *I think it's different concrete here*,
the mother remarked, first foray onto your streets
when I was but a bud, not yet seasoned, blank canvas,

yet to be broken (in).

Green spots, French follies, as if to pardon all
that had been cut down, like us; the spectators
from the fall when the streets had already moved

on to a damp summer.

* *Habillé* is the French word for dressed- he was dressed in...

LA MÈRE ET LE PETIT OISEAU

for The Mother

Sometimes the weakest are tossed out before their time, as if to test.
When you're the only one raised in a bed of beginnings collected from other trees
you have to push yourself out
or stay and choke.

Young bird flees nest
and no twig is long enough to bring him back.

I think it's different concrete here, you said
when you came to collect observations of the new nest
as if considering the comfort of the ground should I fall so far from origin.

You pushed beak bitterly against *the wrong twigs,*
thinner twigs, foreign twigs you'd never felt against your feathers,
clawing at curiosities in the cracks
as if Paris's plumage needed pruning.

When you finally stopped flapping and dusting
and sticking shiny bits of tat into my early efforts at housekeeping
I took you, one evening,
to the top of the tallest metal tree
and drew for you a map of all the flights I'd planned to take
and showed you places I'd left markers to guide me home.

La Mère et le Petit Oiseau means The Mother and the Little Bird

Deuxième Partie: The Living

WHEN CONSIDERING WHAT TO WEAR

You were papered over in such pomp and circumstance,
such a marvelling in the rigidity of centuries since removed

but I found, as we peeled back each other's layers
that breath lingered behind all that had built up around us.

Naked can be the hardest choice to make
though the most comfortable when meticulously considered.

QUAI SAINT-MICHEL

I came to imprint evolution over older interpretation
in a city still reliant on its first canvas,

a decoupage of the ramblings of a modern-day man
cutting into the concept of form next to les Bouquinistes-

sellers of decaying ideals in dying books by the banks
of the Seine whose levels rose every year as if nature

was trying to drown out all that had not yet diminished.
A rose is not just a window of cut glass

reflection is not always concerned with all that is current.
I'd cast you in memory as stone-cold until one night-

a manifestation by les Pont des Arts, coming ever closer
to the water. You tortured us, I'd thought, till the river

ran under and in its reflection I caught your shadow.
In child-thinking mind I'd cast you as impenetrable rock,

but you were fool-hearted, stubborn stance of a lost boy,
sticking plasters over suggestions of any openings.

---

* *Les Bouquinistes* are booksellers along the Seine, who sell used and
antiquarian books, photographs and magazines from their green wooden
boxes built into the riverbank, not far from the rose, stained-glass window of
Notre Dame.

OBITUARIES

You loved watching football and found joy in the obituaries;
the lines of life after it was lost. You liked watching the news,

thrived at washing the car, in that driveway, every Saturday
and again on Sunday, after handing out the missal at mass,

scrubbing it over and over, as if soap and suds could erase
the truth of everything you couldn't clean off your own skin.

You liked washing the car and watching the news and noting
neighbours from behind the blinds, you found joy in papers;

the trials and trivial things that happened before they posted
your obituary and I wondered how you'd felt about your own.

I was in Paris at the time and never opened the black and white
paper that imprinted on your fingertips to see if it told the truth

of who you were or if, like the car and curiosities of those close,
it had been washed clean of who it was you never wanted to be.

PROMISES MADE AT LOMBARDS

That haunting, that dance;

we brushed soft shoe against hard surface,
the pre-millennium stream of slow smoke;
jazz notes under low lights down at Lombards
with its wine by the bottle so that we swayed
to those notes too complicated to catch hold of.

We were saxophones, playing pink elephants
between the duke's darkness and the white lights
of the blinding dawn. Prisoners to the poison,
we stepped across that floor, already haunted,
devouring desire before it was kissed by the ghost

we'd promised each other not to shake.

Previously appeared in the pamphlet *In the Jitterfritz of Neon*

*Le Duc des Lombards is one of the most famous Jazz Clubs in Paris,
located in Chatelet, whose theme is derived from a jazz symphony by Duke
Ellington called Black, Brown and Beige.

GEORGES

Colour,
he saw colour,
in a park, a simple park,
on a Sunday, colour captured in the summer.

Colour,
he painted colour,
in that park, clear, considered,
untampered colour, specs of colour,
rays of light, in a park, on a Sunday, in the summer,
in a season of details, in a salon of specifics, under demands to co-operate.

Colour,
he saw colour,
a canvas of light and colour,
a carnival of colour in a park, on people;
simple people, working people, fishing people,
fidgeting people, not polished people, not posh people.

They
buried him,
in a park, another park,
a quieter park, still with colour and light.
They buried him and then they buried his son and then
another. Life. Then death. Father and sons. Children and all that art.

but only art survived.

*George Seurat painted Un dimanche après-midi à l'Île de la Grande Jatte/A Sunday afternoon on the island of La Grande Jatte between 1884 and 1886 on this narrow island on the edge of Paris. He died in 1891. He was 31. His son died two weeks later. His second child died during or just after birth. He is buried in Père Lachaise cemetery in Paris.

FIESTA, EST-CE QUE CE MONDE EST SERIEUX?

Hemingway loved the bull, both the beast and the shit;

the bravado of animal instinct bared on horny streets
in heat, caught up, breathless, in the chase; the *Aficionado*
on fire, at the Fiesta, those *buenos hombres* who always knew
how to get a bed in a hotel with not a single room left to rent

and then the beast;

galloping through fools
to freedom in the sweltering sun,
under buckling balconies with crowds who knew the clause

freedom was not a prize in waiting within the ring
as the rockets roared
and the costumes and cape commenced.

Far from the fiesta, in France, in the 5th, I'd stop sometimes
as the scent of fevered breath brushed past cheek, unable to catch it,
and itch, later, as if sand was caught in the curve of my collar.

Hemingway loved the bull...

*Ernest Hemingway, whose autobiography *A Moveable Feast* opens with the lines 'If you
are lucky enough to have lived in Paris as a young man, then wherever you go for the rest
of your life, it stays with you, for Paris is a moveable feast,' lived for a time in 1920's in
Paris in the 5ème arrondissement, not far from the Irish College and my first steps at
exploration. This poem was inspired, in part, by La Corrida, a song by Francis Cabrel

32, RUE DU MOULIN VERT

Léo,

she yelled, between the brush strokes
in the basement every day, the magnolia
trembling in the shade, an everyday actress
trying out new roles of mother, wife, lover,
writer, painter, capturing time on a canvas
while the kids grew forever out and up and

off.

Leo, she yelled, in a voice that trembled,
knowing he might not answer back, one day.
Some days we just said *Bonjour. Ça va. Mais oui.*

A plus!

On other days, as she poured me coffee
I never liked but never refused, she stirred
time with sprinklings of settled dust under
which lay clippings of her youth on film,
in the press, pressed down in between
the strained pages no one else cared to caress.

Leo,

she'd yell, into the garden, growing ever wilder
and most days he'd come. A few times, she called
my name and I too would run to her light,
ever flickering, just like a bulb about to blow.

PARIS IS BURNING

I've sat and watched smoke slip
from my lips, like it's that simple
to let out all we've taken in.

Echoes now, on this street
where once there were windmills,
where once I wished for smoking to cauterize
all that time hadn't taken from the tongue.

Smoking, at older vantage point,
the scent of nicotine nudging nostrils,
tinged with all the things
this city once brought to lips.

THE HISSING IN THE SUMMER

Summer,
after last night's thunder
and slow comes the sigh. Summer,
running down the back of spring's bonds
like snakes on the sliver,
through this strangled city,
crawling out from under last season's weeds
onto fresh lawns, coveting form
on giddy grasses tumbling towards a fall.

Summer slithers
in between these blocks of concrete
that cannot sustain the heat while I wait,
without the appease of a single breeze,
for Spanish lips to defy all that is a stone certainty;
every season has its downfall, every summer
a skin soon to be shed

I'm not his, he's not mine,
he's not hers, we do not belong together,
we are not compliments,
we don't have room for the other outside of want,
like this city of stars that should not contain the sun.
We are serpents, hissing on borrowed sheets.

Summer leaves us burnt,
with echoes of all we could not contain
like the cords he strummed that were made to cut,
like all we tasted of each other,
like those nights of smoking skins and second-hand laughter
when we were players, in parks,
looking for stars in between the sunlight.

98, BOULEVARD DU MONTPARNASSE

We met often,
          on Sundays, too old for *La Coupole*
but nostalgic enough for a slow seat at *Le Select,*
wondering if it was Hemingway or our own Beckett
who'd left the brolly on the stand;
                an unclaimed link to a time
now meandered into myth like we were; at times
together, apart, same road but different direction,
coming in to catch up over cuisine
                    as traditional
as the easy step of their formal waiter who oozed
professional but held friendly for the others, after.
We sipped on selected Sundays,
          quelques coupes de champagne
amid the outdated gentry with quaffs and curled
moustaches and curious colognes, sitting next to
history hunters who wondered
              where Picasso sat
and was the light right on their profile, just in case.
We too came in curious with odd colours, cords
we'd been curating
            in our sketchbooks,
curious as to whether someday someone would
wonder where we sat, would wonder if we were
the owners of all those brollies
           they wanted to grab hold of
in the hope they'd feel the weight of a purpose.
We met often, on Sundays, always sandwiched in
between the heavy courses

of foie gras
and côtelettes d'agneau and sipped champagne
while we served each other accounts of our own
liaisons and watched to see
if one aroused the demand of a dessert.

* *La Select* and *La Couple* are two restaurants, famous for former clients
like Ernest Hemingway, Samuel Beckett and F. Scott Fitzgerald.

CHRISTMAS IN SOMEONE ELSE'S SHIRT

Christmas came with cosy discomfort; the clutter, the chaos
and the crowds growing greedy in the Galeries Lafayette

under distraction of dome and the wonder of how any tree
of such weight could hang from such height, so far from root.

We kissed in someone else's shadow, whispered in absence
of his voice. You poured Absinthe into glasses too small

to be of use and didn't blink when I complimented his cologne
on the shirt you gave me, afterwards. Later, I lay on his pillow

and felt a breath judging the weight of my stay from a distance
that was only temporary, like the shadow I left on those sheets

in that too big bed where our two tiny bodies felt so crowded
amid all its soils, like on metro no. 9, direction Marie d'Ivry,

on a Saturday, in December when breaths smelt of Raclette
and Ricard and all the rest that are only ever seasonal scents.

*Every Christmas, Galeries Lafayette department store has an enormous
Christmas tree, often made up of hundreds of smaller trees hanging above the
customers heads from its famed stained-glass ceiling. *Raclette* is a firm winter
French favourite, originating in Switzerland, comprising of a tabletop grill where
guests have individual mini pans where they melt their cheese and add whatever
accompany they desire like cured hams and vegetables.

Troisième Partie : The Loving

TEMPORARY THINGS

after Au Chat Noir

Listen, she said, *delicious can die young, enough can come without a warning,*
a scratch doesn't always leave a scar, eternity is a temporary thing. And I heard.

Now I store moments in between the pages where I once pressed
flowers as the nights devour the stars bleeding their way through

this clawing space. Time is temporary but experience counts for eternity.
Even in basements, bleeding can be beautiful. I sip from the saucer

of liquid lovers, soon to be ghosts lost to scent, who'll pour me in poetry
after we've penned the ending I'll sing of in the beatnik of the black cat.

I'll lay, carefully, those meanders along these lines, lives that sparked
a flame before moving on to the meniscus of someone else's milk.

*Au Chat Noir is a bar, restaurant and home to Spoken Word Paris; a venue for poetry and
performance every Monday in the 11ème arrondissement.

FOR A MOMENT, MID-AFTERNOON

He arrived
on a Monday, the mid-afternoon had passed
and the pouring of a full red a possibility. He
was lounging on the sofa by the second glass,
his head on the pillow of my lap, telling tales
of red stones
stretched out like fine flesh along the scorched
soil of his southern city. We met at the market
on Rue Daguerre while I wondered how long
the berries would last and he; such suggestion
amid a swamp
of freshly fermenting frowns. Later that day,
in an unexpected blush of spring, our tongues
tickled the full-bodied red in steamed glasses
as if everything north had finally found flame.
After he left Paris
and my bed in the apartment with its shutters
which echoed of his south, I sat cross-legged
on that sofa, still damp, teasing my lips with
the last sip of wine, regarding his empty glass
where he'd left it
in the middle of the floor when we'd moved
for a moment, to the shade of the bed. We
spoke again, once, a longing on a phoneline
amid a hot summer Paris couldn't cope with,
I was naked
on that empty bed as he drank beer *au terrace*
down south again, his bare feet teasing those
red-hot stones.

11, AVENUE DU PRESIDENT WILSON

Sometimes it was that simple;
lines that guide you where to lie
beneath the fluidity of the flesh.

Sometimes the frame does not fit;
a canvas can be pulled too tight to comfort,
the form does not cooperate to hospital corners.

We lunge at desire but lie about that too,
strike poses to appear pure in our posture

but we are prostitutes;
selling the slices of ourselves we cannot swallow.

Sometimes, it was that simple;

you on your back, me on my knees, you turning over, me;
looking for the way out

but caught in lines too cold to be constrained within a frame.

Sometimes I sat in a musée on a Sunday
wondering how the model felt
when master moulded him into something else.

DECLAREZ VOTRE FLAMME

Ripened Nancy-boy new to rue des Archives,
scent of the flesh finally in flame, names
cannot drown you after you've learnt to swim;
faggot only an edging now to wear on the cuff.

Paris is a partnership in the early days of courtship;
learning how to cultivate an appetite for beauty
despite the concrete corners its histories have taught
to cut into a diamond that can never be set,

learning how to hold, how to be held, understanding
when to plead for more and how to say enough
before one is left to bleed while the left bank
illuminates above the final droplets of inspiration.

You do not tame the beast but climb your way
cautiously to the top, on occasion, like Eiffel did
when every Parisian party pronounced him crazy;
demanding submission to that overgrown erection.

Now they can't get enough
but always err on the edge of aloof.

Early on, it was about being seen in places of select;
à la terrace in Saint Germain with the slow service
of *Les Magots* while lighting liaisons with Gauloises
sans filtre. Later, with sex less Pigalle performance

and more interesting observation from *The Pompidou,*
we moved east, where she once sang of those regrets
we never considered, while lying breathless au Buttes
Chaumont, with our tongues plunged into every folly.

In the beginning, aux Archives, we evaded documents
in beatnik basements, crawling closer to the definition
of everything that turned into nothing, like Nancy
names that never drowned but later, above ground,

we hung away fancied faggoted cuffs to open diaries
as if we were all Nins and you, Paris, smirking like
a Miller we thought we could never have enough of.
Nubile Nancy-boy new to des allumettes, the scent

of flesh, finally in flame.

* *Rue des Archives* (street of the archives) is a street is *Le Marais*, home to many gay bars and
restaurants. *Allumettes* is the French word for matches. Anaïs Nin was the famous diarist who
dated novelist Henry Miller in Paris in the 1930's. *Les Deux Magots* is a famous restaurant
with a terrace in the rather chic Saint Germain section of the 6ème arrondissement.
Pompidou refers to the modern art gallery *Centre du Georges Pompidou* in the 1er
arrondissement. *Buttes Chaumont* is a hilly park of many follies on edge of Paris, in the
19ème arrondissement, to the east, more homely and less touristy and shiny where Edith Piaf
was born who sang of No Regrets (Non, je ne regrette rien)

41, BOULEVARD DE STRASBOURG

Sometimes
I tear photos from magazines and paste them
onto my skin to remind me of things forgotten.

A decoupage
I thought this body would be; a mash-up
of non-chronological chaos, tattoos of eating storms
that told of everything I'd stopped to touch.

I remember
waking on a Sunday above the *Boulevard de Strasbourg,*
feathers in a doomed fight on the far side of the glass-
a storm I couldn't get quite close enough to touch.

We still oozed of soured Gin Fizzes from *La Tropic*
and somewhere, in the back of my senses, I still smell
a *Sandwich Grec*, rotting.

That was one of the first things I pasted onto flesh
and one of the first things, years later, I noticed
distance had removed

as I descended from a train in *Gare du Nord*
and watched the rain bash against glass

I was finally on the other side of.

---

* Le Tropic Café was a cocktail bar in Châtelet in the 1er arrondissement
serving the best Gin Fizzes at the end of the 1990's, perfect after catching a
movie in the confusion of the subterranean shopping mall of *Les Halles.*

AU CANAL SAINT-MARTIN

Samedi, c'était pour le sport au canal Saint-Martin
in the shimmer of the grey concrete shivering on the water
that appeared often unaware of its direction

but on we ran, both breathless, nonetheless reckless
in our rush to get out of those beds
that were not made to hold us for so long.

Saturday, was for training at Canal Saint-Martin
trying to see how far a stone could be tossed free
before it sank below the stream,

the current doesn't always carry, a bite doesn't always bleed,
being broken doesn't mean you lay down and die;

there are other ways to be bent;

fucking shadows against mirrors
that knew who I was once before illusion dissolved
in those waters, sinking under all that concrete.

Samedi, c'était pour le sport.

Samedi, c'était pour le sport means Saturday, it was for sport.

IN PARIS, A PAIR, TASTING

We ate late, always,
dinner a meal of plucked observations
as much to titillate as to taste.

We devoured each other, always,
before dessert added too much sweetness
to our combative copulations.

Sometimes I pressed my mouth
so hard against your lips
that you'd have to swallow your own words.

Sometimes

when we weren't hungry
we'd sit in the back of the darkness, in silence,
running our hands along each other's bodies

to see if it made it any easier
to hear what the other was trying to say.

SOME SCENES WE ARE STUCK WITH

the hold of that hand in the taxi as we left a city
I hadn't said goodbye to and you;
latching on to something that hadn't been formed.

Some scents are forever tied to necks
where we've left the lie of our lips

like you said, yesterday, when I found you
crossing back over, after so long on the other side
and the first thing you mentioned was my scent,

still that scent.

Some things latch on like limbs and I wonder
if you will sniff, still, when I slip you from my spotlight
as another taxi carries me off.

DIVING IN AT QUAI DE LA SEINE

Je t'aime,
tu sais, you said, à la terrasse
where divers jumped into worn water
that wasn't even warm anymore.

Dégueulasse, I thought, how willing we are
to slip into currents others already caressed;
his stream, her flow, their bath, those breasts
waiting at turned tables to be tasted,
seats still stained with the scent
of the previous participant's perspiration.

Je t'aime, tu sais, you said, on that terrasse
as couples climbed out of the cinema
and let go of hands; holds the darkness
held so much easier than the cold
light tossed back from those worn waters
of Villette's basin where divers descended
into things previously tasted.

Je t'aime, tu sais, you said, and I, embarrassed
by a lost breath, held my chest
as if something was reaching down inside
to pull out the air from the organ
while you glanced around at other tables
with other offerings. *Je t'aime,* you said.
Je sais.

*At the waterside terrasse café, next to MK2 cinema, at Le Bassin de
Villette, the walls are filled with quotes from movies like *Je t'aime* and
Dégueulasse; the French word for disgusting. *Tu Sais* means You know and
Je sais means I know

44

LES CATACOMBES

Gold glitters best undercover, diamonds only friends
after pressure and how we shone under all that weight.

Je t'aime, tu sais, you said and you did; light pressure
on lips, against hips, intoxication licked before trick,

before the chisel came to be the holder of your hand
and the pressure of all that had started out as lithe

began to pound. They say gold glitters best undercover
and you drowned yourself; like a teenager discovering

her first passion for perfume and the rest left to choke.

I remember the first time, slipping underground,
Denfert dissolving as I went down and you undressed,

you always wanted to be naked, to peel back the fabric,
sever the skin, burn a light into the void of all things dead,

press it tightly to see if it came back to life; pressure,
not perish. You were never good at letting go, moving on.

Downstairs you whispered *je t'aime* again, below the light,
grinding it down, with the hope of uncovering a diamond.

*Les Catacombes is a series of underground passageways, with an entrance
at Denfert Rochereau, in the 14ème arrondissement, which leads to an
ossuary housing the bones of bodies dug up from the cities overcrowded
cemeteries. They were moved, under the cover of night, during the 1780's.
It opened as a museum in the 1874.

9, RUE ÉMILE DUBOIS

While you were looking down
from above, trying to pick out
those perfect particles from all
that passed through us, I tried
to understand how time moved

right around us; how your desire
became my taste, how my books
turned out to be holders of dust
on all your shelves next to round

mirrors I'd screwed into your square walls on slow Parisian
Sundays opened only to the boulangeries and Mr. Bricolage,

how the reflections they held
of who we were to each other
never looked that comfortable
in the centre of the final frame.

SOME PEOPLE THAT WE USED TO BE

We sit now and sip cocktails, the waiter pulls out your chair
and hands me the menu after calling you madame.

I strain now to hear your voice; softer, gentler,
feminine finding freedom.

I catch you checking your lipstick in the mirror, pulling a curl
back into place above those blushed cheekbones

still a little swollen, a normal evening in August, in Paris,
sipping gins and rums and telling tales,

swapping tables in Korean restaurants that give us a brief taste
of who it was that we used to be.

We sit over cocktails; the man and the madame, looking like a couple
in the reflection of the tainted mirror

and I wonder can anyone tell, as you smooth out your skirt,
that you used to be my boyfriend.

SUNSET KISSES

after the photograph Le Baiser de l'Hôtel de Ville by Robert Doisneau

Sombre moods on Saturdays,
these sunsets, so serious
as if each was the last, as if we were too late.

Moody blues in black and white,
love is not for the lonely, even the Seine can separate.

Memory can be a curse,
the water does not always wash away
enough, suffit!

Ça suffit!

That kiss was caught on camera
as if forever was affordable, as if you can capture perfection
in a place that perishes, even the café has closed.

The kiss was only a concept,
just enough of a lie of the lens, kept alive
on lips of courting couples, copying all they cannot hold.

Degrees of affection
that can shiver, after the shot.

* *Ça suffit* is French for That's enough.

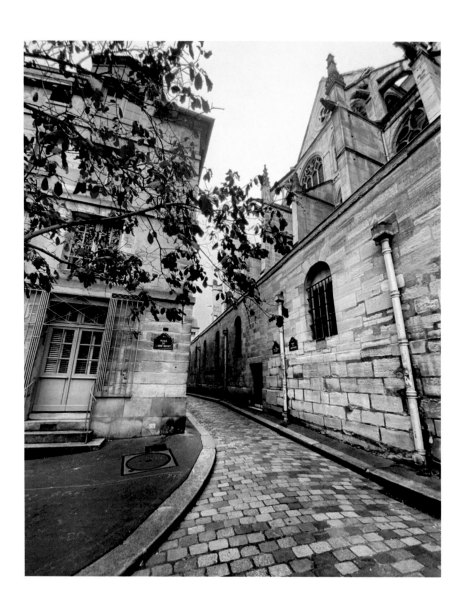

Quatrième Partie: The Moving

LE PARFUM DE LA JEUNESSE

Walkways of dog shit and metros that open into underground
pathways of piss, narrow stairwells of nicotine-knotted railings

and those croissant crumbs squashed into cornered crevasses,
two-legged dogs on tiptoes licking it large while their pit-bulled

four-legged fancies in diamond chokers hump deserted scooters
in middle paths of main streets and yet we come just like cattle

into the chaos, munching our way from the farms of everywhere
else to the stench of what we have now come to identify as cult;

conditioned in cold cannisters; 19 square meters and shit squatting
in posh toilettes with paper towels that can tear through any crack.

Concrete does not have a lasting scent, it doesn't even rot, so we
paint it with dimensions it can never contain; like the yellow brick

road, once diversions from witches that were never really wretched.

KIDS ON THE COBBLES

You wore a fur coat; a found object from the 70's the 90's
had yet to distinguish as disgusting. Funny, you; vegetarian
before we knew how to swallow a full vegan and virginal too,
tumbling from tight tops and velveteen bottoms that left pals

panting while you fingered white keys in beatnik basements
that hardly held us and then toppled later, across the cobbles
while deciphering all the cautious questions of who you were,
who you thought I was and who we'd never be to each other.

I wonder, from this far side of that ocean that holds no trace
of any way back in its make-up, if our whispers are still there;
Right Bank, behind the gay bars that thrilled us on Saturdays
and those Jewish bakeries that filled us on Sunday mornings

after waking up, alone. There are many things I wanted to say
and didn't, and other things I did that I never got to take back,
but we were just kids, too young to see how we lived in a city
where every little thing that happened was already set in stone.

BOY SO BLUE

In a park in Paris, France, kids outgrow the trees they're climbing
and the birds; busy their feathers in flights of unassuming freedom.

In between the battle and bustle, I fall up through stilled thoughts
as someone tickles strings on cords still too distant to be defined,

hunting for the key to harmony, probably and guarding their guitar
from the bright lights of that starless sky as if they know, already,

how celebrity will one day come down to cripple all their creativity.
A blackbird comes to call, looking for crumbs cast off, rummaging

for a refuge, like we all do, desperate for a distraction from circling
sun and shining skins blistering under the bland and all its blander.

Sitting in a park in Paris, France, torn in a trance, from 22 to 42,
coming back to recall how I first found favour in exploring you;

two rooms, no light, we became masters of the Marais; two simple
singletons, senselessly sinking innocence into the marshes, cavorting

over its cobbles, courting kisses of single sparks, climbing our way
up and over the losses we thought at the time to be insurmountable

disasters. But they were just dances, like the tiny birds and climbing
kids, prances we perform, up and under, over and through. We are

all birds, flirting with honesty and invisibility under a sweltering sun,
sometimes recalled, sometimes forgotten before begun. Sitting here,

in a park in Paris, France, trying to understand messages in melodies
and to comprehend the cords forged in the flesh of the boy so blue.

*Inspired by the song California and many other cords and tunes by Joni Mitchell

STILL MOVING ON METROS

Moments on the metro, still moving,
still cruising, still choosing, still cosy
with commuters not communicating,
commuter looks like communication
but no commuter communicates.

Moments on the metro, still moving,
still breaking, still stopping at stations
where beggar enters with la chanson,
trying to get his chance on, prancing in
to pockets of passengers losing patience
with moments on metros, still moving,

still making manoeuvres along carriages
of commuters consumed with new tunes
on cool phones and hand-held computers
and fold away scooters as cute girl eyes
gay guy in grey shirt while another guy
notices the mini of her skirt and dreams
of dessert, dreams of slithering so slow
along her carriage, to drive his tiny train
into her station, like he was Spartacus,
the Thracian, riding illusion's vibration.

Moments on the metro, still moving,
still chancing, still stealing odd glances
between penning poems and nodding
into naps with bags loaded onto laps
of madams with makeup, making faces
as if painting Picassos, checking mirrors
to see if the eyes line up. Lines of metros
still moving, still tearing through tunnels
of non-communicative commuters;
cool, classy, crazy, quirky and the man
smelling of starvation and stale streets

and blackened feet, buskers belting
out bad notes and getting worse looks
instead of crisp notes, the red hat
with that short skirt, the tall ones,
the tired ones, the tourists plotting
their positions on plans too small
to be able to even pinpoint a pub.

Metros, making their way through
moments between the darkness
on tracks all laid and loyal not like
our thoughts; spinning and fretting
about fitting; fitting on, fitting in,
fitting into trains, tracks and skirts,
holes, cyber lives to make us whole,
in private compartments to crush us
closer into strangers, coming closer
to scents and smells and stenches
that choke us, the breaths breathing
onto the backs of tensed-up necks
of unnamed neighbours slithering
like snakes on tracks taking us back
& forth, to & fro; to work, to home,
to him, to her, to zero, to the passing
parties and improbable possibilities.

Moments on the metro, still moving
through this underground, under
the ground, under cars and bikes and
feet walking and the taxis swerving
and cursing at bikes and pedestrians
crossing the wrong way on the wrong
side as straight rain falls into puddles
over gutters while water trickles down
from the daylight into darkness, into
the tunnels where it finds us with our
moments on the metro, still moving.

24, RUE DE MENILMONTANT

You tore down a ceiling to see the stars
before packing up discarded parts in the attic
and blocking out the light by leaving it there,
in cases of clutters.

You were always crafty.
I should've known from the beginning, after renting
and you becoming a regular. You kept returning,
settling yourself into my new armchair in your old home,
your feet retracing steps in their former space.

You were German,
playwright displaced in Paris, in love with the quarter's
shifty shops, all selling bulk on the cheap, those places
that always had trouble correctly spelling brand names.

I'd find you there,
when I'd come home, drinking your crafty way
through my red wine, pressing your feet down
into the tommettes, pasting all your ideas in between
the cracks in the walls, the holes you had never told me
the truth about until it was too late, until they tumbled
down like the assurance of a cheapskate.

* *Tommettes* are hexagonal floor tiles, often found under carpets in old
Parisian apartments

CIMETIERE PERE LACHAISE

I see you bolting
through the boulevards, taller than before, than when I wore
you, when we wore each other down into cobbles that now cut.

I am returned,
could not keep away. Our skin is elastic, it stretches out so far
till we forget where we pinned it down. Then comes the recoil.

The sun doesn't only burn
the closer you come to it, the moon doesn't only control time,
here, heat is stored in concrete so we are burnt before burial.

Here, in this cemetery
the earth is open, they come to listen, to wonder if Edith sings
as they leave flowers, leave her flowers and watch them dying

like she was in her day;
a single sparrow reaching out for a tune under all that darkness.
I live just across from the spot where they think she was born,

under a lamp light
having fallen out too soon or her mother getting down too late.
We're the stuff of myth, we leave you roses but don't even know

if you liked the flower.
The shadow's shifted in this peculiar park where you can't run
or drink but you can take pictures of all that's no longer there,

you can leave kisses,
if you are not caught, on the concrete wit of Wilde, on a hill,
in the 20ème arrondissent, to the east of this bereaved city,

a hill rising higher and higher from bones we're crawling over
where I see you at times, a shadow of who we were, shifting.

ÇA SUFFIT!

I remember rainstorms
and running through straight lines
flooding cobbled streets,
laughter carries louder under brollies
rises and falls back onto heads, onto faces,
onto mouths like that rain, like lips,
like tongues that taste of sweat and surrender
and something indescribable,
that tiny space we save for later
when we admit to knowing, while running,
that something was always missing.
I remember rainstorms
and running through all those shut Sundays
of grey roofs and terracotta pots
on steps that collected rain drops
as if it knew already
how much memory meant after, later,
when the sun came out
and there were no more brollies to keep us together.
I remember rainstorms
and running along all those boulevards
as if they were battlefields
and the droplets were bullets
and I couldn't remember
how to say *that's enough* in French.

DESTINY, SOMETIMES FAR FROM FABULEUX

after the film *Le Fabuleux Destin d'Amélie Poulain*

It had dwindled slightly, upon return, how quickly attraction fades
afterwards, in the afterglow of so much naked, growing discomforts,

wondering how to lie your way out of the sheets and onto the streets.
It had withered slightly, upon return; all the wonder turned to weight.

All those stones she had skimmed along Saint Martin sank, eventually.
Not everything remains fabuleux, there isn't an Amélie on every street

thinking about Lady Di and painting paths for the blind after the crack
of a crème brûlée. It had faded, slightly, upon the return; all of that gilt

turned greedy in Montmartre, now tourist trapped and flattened down
by the pressure of fame, smothered by kick of Can-Can and its price

which now says can-not! It had aged, in the end, into something more
sedate, something to be admired for what it was, once, a stained relic

whose shiny surfaces once bounced with tossed stones when painters
were Picasso's and the hills filled with the windmills and green fairies

and stuff and nonsense, when its writers couldn't afford to buy letters
in order to spell the word cliché. It had dwindled slightly, upon return.

EVEN IN THE FINAL FALL THERE CAN STILL BE A SPARKLE

I sit in between streets,

in between ageing and learning,
learning to forget and trying to remember,
eating time before it's cleared away as people pass

some looking and leaning,
not knowing I'm soon to be leaving,

not noting I've already been removed from the menu,

replaced in his city
of time forgotten thoughts;

what we heard last night
at the kiss of Buttes-Chaumont, former quarry,
now a folly; an echo, only, of the applause already appeased.

Dig it up and you're left with a gaping hole.

The bridges here hold seats for only shadows now,
standing in fading light; trickling dust in their final flutter,

see the sparkle of their fall;

an acknowledgement of what grounded us together
and covered us over, here, on these streets
my shadow is slowly slipping from

as I sit, in between.

Cinquième Partie: The Leaning Out

THAT WHICH IS MAPPED OUT AT THE START

There was always an end
even before we started
to circumnavigate
time's tock.
Listen

still,
hear it
winding back
to that first tick.
There was always an end.

BETTER THAN

after Leonard Cohen and Jardin des Serres d'Auteuil which rest next to Roland Garros

Better than huge genitalia
is something I can cup comfortably
in the palm of my hand,
I cannot spend all day
riding that tower Eiffel left us-
hard and cold like a corpse
and often, in the evening,
ambivalent to competing stars
it tries to squash with the slim prick
of its furthest reaching point.

Better is the slow undress
of bud into begonia
under glass of heated house
whose reflection catches all falling stars
to the west of all that is no longer
the centre of anything
other than history,
next door to where they hit
brightly coloured balls
back and forth

all
day
long!

*Jardin des Serres d'Auteuil is a botanical garden, situated on the edge of
Bois de Boulogne, next to Roland Garros tennis courts, dating back to
Louis XV in 1761, and currently home to greenhouses built at the end of
the 1800's producing over 100,000 plants per year. There have been
attempts to replace the garden and glasshouses with more tennis courts.
The newest glasshouses were built in 2019 around the edges of the
Simonne Matthieu court.

REPERCUSSIONS

Standing in former shadows, in someone else's rain sinking deeper
into skin I've slipped from, having learned how it felt to be trapped.

I never needed to be better, to be able to discuss Sartre over salad.
Standing in former shadows, grown over and older as the echo

of our fingers strumming that slow song refilled a space that time
had slipped into storage, next to that red room where I'd touched

parts of you before I came to you and you came over all the parts
of me we later left bleeding. Some cords are so simple to pull off

while others have repercussions. Were we always courting crazy?
We could never be just one note, one skin, one shadow, one city.

TAKEN

What to report? To what port do you swim,
in how little can you drown? Shallow is often
sister to shady, air is not anything until it's nothing

and nowhere. Sometimes existence is acknowledged
only in disappearance. Fear is not anything until it's
everywhere and everywhere. Skin does not tingle until

it's been touched or torn. But is there a light, still,
at the back of the darkness of the ransacked room
where they found you choking? I tried to report it all

but trust, once taken, cannot be listed as something
stolen on any part of a single Parisian police report.

LOOKING FOR YOUR LOST ENCOURAGEMENT

It takes a single stoke of stupidity
to strike a match beneath a sky
of stars and expect to be seen.

The second time I returned I didn't
smoke anymore but my lips eventually
grew dry to taste, my fingers recalled
a fondness for a fag and, as I pulled in
you turned to catch a brighter star.

Love is a fickle find, like a match
blowing out at the slightest sign
of dissension within the pack.

SLOW MOVING SORROW, FRIDAY 13TH

November 2015

In a supermarket, on a Saturday, in the 14ème,
on the 14th, in numb November, in Paris,

their Paris, our Paris, my Paris,

people push grief in comfortless trolleys
down shadowed aisles of silence,
strangers, claiming their spaces

in queues of slow-moving sorrow,
a sorrow for what we lost behind the light.

In a supermarket, in the 14ème, on the 14th,
as the numbers rise on a Saturday morning
there is nothing available on a single shelf

to fill the void of what we lost in the night.

SOME THINGS OPEN FOR A REASON

November 2020

I wrote of slow-moving sorrow, once, in November,
on a dull day in November when it should have rained,

a Saturday in the supermarket where we pushed trollies
down aisles that held everything that would eventually

perish and nothing to replace what we'd lost in the night.
All of us in a supermarket, a fraternity of frightened folk

looking for ways to restock. Time turns and we're tribes;
nodding to neighbours unknown, taking note of people

passing, of men on the metros next to us, across from us,
watching us, watching them watching, wishing to be seen

before it's too late. People fucked more, later, afterwards,
looking for ways to carve the emptiness out of the inside,

as if a tongue or a finger or any old cock could revive
all that had since been expired. Eventually we grew tired,

of shopping, fucking, carving bigger holes into our voids.
Eventually, after all the hours and the days and the weeks

we took Polyfilla to all that had been emptied of ourselves,
filling in the parts that for a time had opened up to change.

HOW THE DUST SETTLES, REGARDLESS OF THE WEATHER

Sometimes the mind forecasts the day's weather first thing
in the morning when I know the plan is for indoor cleaning;

rehousing dust on cupboard tops that only this mind imagines.
Age wages worry onto things that don't concern the moment,

meanwhile, midway through, I'm trying to learn to stress less
about the next breath, trusting the brain to pacify the panic.

Pace. Pause. Peace. Let dust settle. Smoking was a distraction
to tension, when sex wasn't available, sometimes it was both;

before, after, in between. Sometimes it was only the cigarette
that you could stamp out quickly when you'd taken the right

amount of it inside you so as to remind yourself just how bad
it was for you. Paris was never embarrassed of smoke or sex.

Occasionally, when she was playful and you; pliable, she'd let
you take her to your lips and you could feel her burning you

out before you'd even brought a tongue to her tit. The French
always moan about the weather, whether you wanted to hear

or not, whether you were outside, drowning, or on the wrong
side of the window to be truly touched. I learned how to panic,

first, in Paris, at the end and sometimes I wonder if it was
because I was leaving that it began or if it had nothing to do

with that at all, like dust on cupboards that we only imagine,
that has nothing at all to do with any worry of the weather.

For now, I'm trying to concentrate only on how things settle.

PROPEL

Bait

Young love wore a black beret
before I even acquired a taste for the garlic.
Desire, in the face of desolation, was the fuel of youth
and knowledge, or lack thereof, its propeller
and I was propelled.

Bliss

Years later I still hold the perfume;
late night, 22, me, him and a motorbike on the cobbles
of the quarter Hemingway had left half parched; Mouffetard
with its *vin du table* and *Sandwich Grec* as I devoured
a leather-clad lover on front of the bright lights
in the dark night that danced like unsinkable stars
along the seine. And I could barely breathe.

Beyond

We cut, much later, at every curve
covered in concrete, I'd been duped
by your solid structure, having let go of the leather,
all that gilding requiring so much guile to be cast upon.
Something fell into the river while we licked the illusion
and, in panic, I lost hold of all translation. We dined out,
finally, on a meal that was as bitter on the palate
as the distance we had come from those bright lights
dancing and, for dessert, we tossed that first desire
into the blades of the propeller.

THE ART OF AN EXISTENTIALIST FOLD

When two things come together they become one
like *ori* when it's pressed into *kami*, but is the one
equals parts of the two that had previously existed?

Within the art of Origami, when you fold a page in half,
that, which was once a square, is forever transformed
beneath the pressure of thumb's press so when corners
come to kiss I wonder if they're regarded as the same page.

Though an elastic is ruled by its recoil, its return results
from what it's learnt by being stretched. It comes back
not to comfort but to confront that which let it go.

I have pictures of you I put away; particles of the past
framed in a portrait of who we were before the spiral
brought me up and out and then back; folded over
and coming in to compare first kiss with this last

but it's not just the pace of this breath that's changed,
we have stretched the elasticity of our connection so far
that it doesn't sit back over the bones how it should.

This crease, pressed down along the centre of who we
once were, is not just a fold. In Japan, origami is where
paper has been folded but kirigami is where the paper

                                        has been cut.

ALL THE WATER CARRIES OFF WITH IT

There will always be a part of me
standing by the water's edge

wondering

how much of us
will be washed away

how deep
it must be to drown

and how long a reflection
can remain a concern to the current.

Sixième Partie The Leaving

LE QUAI DE MEGISSERIE

There's a part of me / there / still
with you / below the bridge / by the river
smiling

There's a part of me / there / still
with the water rushing / time flowing / by the bridge
drowning

There's part of you / in me / still
regardless of time / breath / bridge / regardless of the water
I drown in

There's a part of you / there's a part of me
still / watching the water / looking for reflections
of where we lost our course.

A SCENT TO SAIL YOU BACK

The lilt of lavender that lingered
long after, by the leaning,
before the Louvre,

the blossom of fallen rain
making its way around
the curve of every cobble,

the seduction of grease
sandwiched into the darkness
of a *grec*, before the dawn,

the sweet consolation of candy floss
cologne that clung to the pillow,
after you'd left.

Sometimes it's that simple;
a scent to sail you back

*At Paris fashion week, Spring 2016, the House of Dior, led by Raf
Simons, set up camp in the courtyard of the Louvre and the outside of their
domed temporary catwalk venue was covered in half a million flowers in all
shades of lavender. A *sandwich grec* is a stable post-clubbing snack, a
French form of the doner kebab, a baguette filled with a grease feast of not
always identifiable meat, covered in chips, best eaten in the dark.

BIRD SONG

I stroll in soft sundown across a gated garden, so far removed
that not even the simple rumble of your name can recall you.

I consider going in to where the light looks neat and named
but a bird calls from a foreign place, from a branch I cannot see.

Sight comes in second after his song; soft and slow and cycling
back on itself like time, tide and the swift recoil of your touch.

Time was never to be our lover, nor the light to be a signal,
nor a name something to define us. Sight comes in second.

I move in circles ever decreasing as faithfully distant moon, itself
ever revolving, comes out to feed. We eat what we can, fuck till

we're full, birds sing of songs from other shores and only when lost
do we permit ourselves to stop, think and finally ask the meaning.

WHEN NOTRE DAME CAME FALLING DOWN

I'd started packing up places and folding them
into pockets of dried time when I saw her burning.
I was to the north of her centre at that time, upwind
of the flames that were already ashes when they reached

my tongue.

I took communion there, years earlier, taking the wafer
onto that tongue that had yet to know the taste of ash.
People came with novenas and cried as the stars turned on
as if caught by the fires below and the river ran black as if

already in mourning. *C'est comme si quelqu'un était mort*

someone said as I pulled tape over another packed box
the river would carry downstream till it forgot its way back.
They all stood there, on that street by the Seine, where
les bouquinistes sold fading books that smelt of death
while the ashes fell upon their heads, their eyes, their lips

and their tongues. And so there we were;

the grieving and the leaving, open-mouthed, desperate
for one last taste of what we had believed to be eternal.

*C'est comme quelqu'un était mort means it's like someone is dead. *Les Bouquinistes* are the booksellers by the banks of the Seine

ŒUFS BROUILLES

You used to bash
thick heel of stilettoed shoe
against thin frame
of metal water heater
mounted over clogged sink
in pinched corner of kitchen
                    at 6am,
less than six feet
from where I slept
and I leapt, every time,
like someone had smashed an egg
into the side of my skull.

I cannot remember
how we made our way
into that apartment,
how many stairs we took
before we turned   in
or where key was placed
in frame of door
since sealed shut.

Now, a million steps
from a doorframe
that has shifted from focus,
                    I wake
with taste of yoke on my lips
and an echo
of all that has since smashed
and wonder of the tiny little pieces
you'd have to paste together
to bring me back
to sight of you
with shoe in hand.

Œufs Brouillés means 'scrambled eggs'

A SHADE CAUGHT IN THE SHADOW

I walk in circles now, following paths forward
that crossover roads once considered.

Time trips onward but no longer is the line straight,
no longer a captive of direct.

This light is lit now like a last lap, here,
in this place once prized

once positioned next to pride on platforms
now too proud to be passed off as plausible.

I'm on the count-down to lift-off while still turning corners
teased with reflections that once shone

with the shade of an old shadow long since shed.
In these circles, I walk now.

THREADS

You caught me unaware, at first, bare threads barely woven
into anything resembling wearable and you;
a city of doormen cast over centuries into concrete.
Only youth can have designs that so outweigh the depth
of that fine red thread wrapped around reason.

Later, older, on the return, I took up position on plinth
and admired at how little I had cracked under the weight
of all your pretentions while noting the dust that had settled
deeper into the crevasse you ignored on your own carcass

like the blind man who wore that red suit to the black-tie ball.

WHEN I LEFT HER, KNOWING

I walk over drying leaves,
crisp tissue freshly fallen under foot
in this season of the fall.

Some things stay attached
while others change their tempo,
turn, take off.

Au revoir, I whispered and you smiled
knowing I'd be back.

8, RUE DES MAUVAIS GARÇONS

I climb the ladder, pick discarded twigs from blocked gutter
at the end of the roof where the slates swayed slightly
in the storm these summer days have set upon us.

Babies grown feathers and flown nests, their beds now
fodder for winds to wash down these grey slates, rotting
and raining into gutters overflowing. Their home now

at the reach of their wingspan and not a chimney on a roof
with gutters now gushing. I lived, once, on the top floor
of a hotel, at the darkest end of December
and the beginning of a whole new breath-

La Rue des Mauvais Garçons, ça commence,
c'est vrai que ce n'est pas la Rue des Bons Enfants.

The balcony, under gutter, was as economical with comfort
as the thin pillows balancing on large lumps in the small bed
but I sat there, in the twinkling of a Christmas morning
in *Tati* jumper and smoked *Gauloises sans filtre*, drinking

champagne I'd nicked from the bar, wondering

where to build my nest among the rooftops I watched
burning unsafe fires in chimneys as clogged as black lungs
and too small to hold even a single fragile feather. I wonder

if someone watches now from a balcony in *le Marais*
or across the grass of Belleville's *rien de rein* and catches
the last twigs of my homes being blown into oblivion.

---

* *Rue des Mauvais Garçons* means street of the bad boys and *Rue des bon enfants* means street of the good children. Belleville and the 20ème is the birthplace of Édith Piaf and her song *Non, je ne regrette rien*. I smoked cheap Gauloises cigarettes with no filters.

MISSING

We were fine filigree
composed of gaping cracks where truths whispered
before the sealant, like those walls in Ménilmontant,
5th floor walk-up
next to Wilde's wings
kissed by those who thought they knew him, walls
where I hung oversized art on top of all the cracks,
as if it was enough

to stabilise a foundation in peril.
Missing

the ghastly glares of your gargoyles, who all knew,
before we parted, how our future would be housed
in a haunting, their stone eyes
porous to the passers-by
and the rain storming their concrete casts. We too
were oblivious to the comings and goings of all else
and ignorant to how much

we passed through each other, like acid rain
unable to survive all that Oscar worthy wit.

GO BACK

You cannot really go back; to return does not mean to rerun.
I recognise these streets, I recall a certain laugh,
a twisted lie, the shrug of an open door

but my footprints have changed.

I cannot find the same sunflower I drew when I was younger
than this youth I cling to and so many of those doors
have now closed and the lies opened out

to be nothing more than lessons.

I cannot go back

the streets now wear shadows
unconnected to the form I've now become.

A STILL LIFE OF SENTIMENTAL ON A WALL

Memory
is a shot of stillness
sealed behind a lens;
a souvenir
of something unseen
until frozen
in frame.

Some
see this
as a season of rust,
of ruin and running,

but for me
there is a freedom
in this fall.

I'll hang you
on other walls,
in other seasons,
you'll hear me
sing
other songs
to other suitors.

It doesn't mean
we never had
a summer,
only that our spring
was too short
to be anything other
than sentimental.

Plan de Paris

LOCATIONS FOR SOME THE POEMS

1er arrondissement
Promises Made at Lombards- Duc des Lombards Jazz Club
Quai de Mégisserie- lined with pet stores in the late 1990's
Quai Saint-Michel

4ème arrondissement
Kids on the Cobbles- rue des Rosiers, Jewish quarter
98, rue Vieille du Temple- apartment building
Lady, Don't Love me Now- 98, rue Vieille du Temple
Œufs Brouillés- 98, rue Vieille du Temple, Le Marais
8, Rue des Mauvais Garçons- Hôtel du Loiret
When Notre Dame Came Falling Down- Cathédrale Notre-Dame de Paris, Île-de-la-Cité

5ème arrondissement
Collège des Irlandais- the Irish College and home to Centre Cultural Irlandais, 5, rue des Irlandais
An Autumn of Amateurs, Medici Fountain- Jardin du Luxembourg
Fiesta, Est-ce que ce Monde est Sérieux ?- rue Mouffetard

9ème arrondissement
Christmas in Someone Else's Shirt- Galeries Lafayette department store, Boulevard Haussmann

10ème arrondissement
41 Boulevard de Strasbourg- apartment building

11ème arrondissement
Temporary Things- Au Chat Noir, a bar and Spoken Word venue, 76 Rue Jean-Pierre Timbaud

14ème arrondissement
98, Boulevard du Montparnasse- La Select, restaurant
Les Catacombes- underground ossuaries in Paris with remains of over 6 million people
9, rue Émile Dubois- apartment building
Slow Moving Sorrow- Monoprix on rue d'Alésia
32, Rue du Moulin Vert- apartment building
For a Moment, Mid-Afternoon- rue Daguerre, street market
62, Rue D'Alésia- La Zeyer, restaurant

16ème arrondissement
11, Avenue du Président Wilson- Musée d'Art Moderne de Paris
Better Than- Jardin des Serres d'Auteuil, botanical gardens situated next to Roland Garros
Georges- île de la Jatte, an island on the Seine

18ème arrondissement
Destiny, Sometimes Far from Fabuleux- Montmartre

19ème arrondissement
Diving In at Quai de la Seine- on a terrace outside the Cinema MK2
Even in the Final Fall there can Still be a Sparkle- Buttes Chaumont, former quarry and now park

20ème arrondissement
24, rue de Ménilmontant- apartment building
Cimetière Père Lachaise- famous cemetery in Paris, home to Édith Piaf, Jim Morrison and Oscar Wilde
Missing- Ménilmontant

PREVIOUS HOMES

Some of the poems have previously appeared, in various formats, in the follow publications for which I am very grateful to everyone involved for giving them a home:

62, rue d'Alesia - 2 Metre Review, Winter Edition 2021
Promises made at Lombards – Neurological Literary Magazine, Oct 2020 & also in the conversational pamphlet with Eilin de Paor, In the Jitterfritz of Neon

41, Boulevard de Strasbourg – Imspired Magazine, Volume 7,Print Volume 2021

Diving in At Quai de la Seine- The Bangor Literary Journal, Issue 14, 2021

When Viewed from within the Frame of Cut Glass - Imspired Magazine, Volume 7, Print Volume 2021

Ça Suffit - Anti-Heroin Chic, Issue 18, 2020

Slow Moving Sorrow, Friday 13th - Nous Sommes Paris, anthology, Eyewear Publishing

When Notre Dame came falling down – Spotlight Poets, Poets Directory

We'll always have... what exactly? - Imspired Magazine, Volume 7, Print Volume 2021

ACKNOWLEDGEMENTS

I would like to start by thanking The Mother, Mona, who understood the need of her only son to fly away at 22, to explore new nests in Paris where this adventure all began. To my family who I love and adore and am constantly inspired by, mainly because they put the D in Drama! Love to all the Donnelly clan.

With love and so many amazing childhood memories to my Riverside family who all were there to see me off in Dublin Airport for that first flight from home; the Tunsteads, the Kerrigans, the Davis clan, the Cahill clan and the McGuirk clan.

I am bound for the rest of my life to be grateful to Mark Davidson, editor of this incredible press that is now family, for giving me the time, space and trust to make this collection. You are a Rockstar with groove firmly installed in your heart.

Enormous thanks to The Arts Council, Ireland for support via the Agility Award which is a tremendous boost to creativity and confidence.

I cannot say enough (pun intended) how fortunate I was to work with Anna Saunders, founder and CEO of the Cheltenham Poetry Festival who was my mentor on this collection. Her guidance, insight, probing and engagement was nothing less than spectacular and this final collection is, in a large part, down to her keen eye that always looked over the pages with an understanding of where I was coming from, where I needed to go and countless pointers for how to get there.

To the Parisian connections that are alive in all of these pages; my thanks to each and every one of you who made these years so important to capture including; Mary and Liam, Ben, Vincent, Yasmine, Abi, Paul, Alice, Shaun, Charlotte, Therese, the entire & Other Stories Atelier and to all the spirits who entered and the other spirits we consumed at Cogun's Café.

I would like to thank the journals and poetry events who have supported me and featured some of the poems from this collection in various forms and other work over the past few years including Black Bough Poetry, Cheltenham Poetry Festival, Flight of the Dragonfly, The Bangor Literary Journal, Anti Herion Chic, Neurological Magazine, Impspired Magazine, Coffin Bell, Fevers of the Mind Press, 2 Metre Review, Eyewear Publishing, Poets Directory, Over the Edge, Fahmidan Journal, Prismatica, Bealtaine, The Adriatic, Barren Magazine, The Runt Magazine, the Ray D'Arcy RTE Radio Show and Catherine Ann Cullen, former poet in Residence at Poetry Ireland for her constantly inspiring work and encouragement on Twitter via her poetry prompts.

I would like to say thank you to the magical Aisling Keogh, Kevin Hynes, Susie Breuer, Saskia Vanderkloot Barre, Gaynor Kane, Eilín de Paor, Rhiannon Howys, Matt MC Smith and Rhona Greene for their light and love.

To my fellow hoglet family here at the Hedgehog Poetry Press, thank you for the support, poetry and inspiration: Gaynor Kane, Nigel Kent, Patricia M Osborne, Julie Stevens, Margaret Royall, Brian McManus, Peter A, Karen Mooney, Vicky Allen, Cathy Carson and Vic Pickup. There are many more and I hope they know who they are.

I would like to say a huge thank you to Community Arts Partnership NI and The Monthly magazine edited by Gordon Hewitt for their enormous support of both my poetry and my poetry podcast Eat the Storms. I would also like to say a huge thank you to all of the guests who have joined me on the podcast. Thank you for ensuring we all Stay Bloody Poetic.

Finally, I would like to give my appreciation for the time and dedication Paul Stephenson, Robert Frede Kenter, Kevin Higgins and Anna Saunders gave to writing the blurbs. It is not an easy task and I am so grateful to each of them whom I admire so much. I am honoured to have their names with me here in this debut full collection.

And to you, the reader, thank you for taking the journey with me. Merci beaucoup. I hope you make it to the end without the need to say Ca Suffit!

"This finely crafted collection takes us on a personal journey to places of love, leaning, longing, and quickly belonging. Richly evocative poems in and of Paris that twist and turn like the narrow staircases of Haussmannian apartment buildings. Studded with literature, painting and cinema, each poem is a portrait of the city in the changing seasons as the young poet sits and sips, drinking in the people and their promise. Donnelly is a romantic who captures the hope and heat of summer, conveys the losses, the strummed cords now cut, the echoes that could not be contained. A sumptuous book of six sequences that offer a linear narrative of having and holding, of latching on, laying down and letting go. Paris gives lessons in love, glitters and sparkles as the poet makes his way across the Seine, over bridges and on the metro, in pursuit of the other, as the sun sets and rises on the City of Lights. Sensual poems that play with slippage and disappearance, repercussions and illusion, as our protagonist, older now, rummages in Sunday markets of memory, sits looking back on crowded squares of desire."

Paul Stephenson, author of *Selfie with Waterlilies* www.paulstep.com

"Damien Donnelly has alighted on the Irish poetry world like an unignorable force of nature over the last little while. His first collection vividly evokes a Paris in which the ghosts of Baudelaire and Frank O'Hara present the reader with a kind of postmodern tango. Long may Donnelly's word dance continue."

Kevin Higgins, author of *Sex and Death in Merlin Park Hospital,* co-creator of *Over the Edge*

"*Enough!* by Damien B. Donnelly, is a beautiful, lyrical, and rhythmic meditation, a testimony to personal 'coming-of-age', a romance and denouncement with startling imagery (the eruptions of desire and anger abound), a Paris of tacky-gaudy tourism, ecstatic desire, philosophical musing and broken love. With its homage/ reference to film, art, architecture, bohemian neighbourhoods, its tropes of Paris and inner-outer geographies, landscapes of self and other situate intricacies of life through memory: its traces, losses, the enjambments of time, place, identity and self-emerging. Via rites of passage, Donnelly's journeys from Ireland to France, in the spirit of Beckett, Joyce, and other sojourners, is a Barthesian voyage of details through a queering lens, a narrative of the poet's developing artistic techniques, an invocation to lovers, and a paean to Donnelly's relationships to art, poetry, the ghosts of history. In rapture, Damien holds the reader's attention. Raptly. A gem of a collection, ecstatic, dreamy, vibrant and brutal by turns."

Robert Frede Kenter, publisher/EIC of Ice Floe Press, author of *EDEN* (Floodlight Editions, 2021), etc.

"The adage 'happiness paints white' is disproved in the vibrant, and richly coloured poems of Damien Donnelley – who, with a painter's eye, offers an exuberant portrait of a life lived fully and with great joy. These are poems that take you to the party, pour you a drink and intoxicate you – they are witty, insightful, highly entertaining and full of compassion, humanity and exhilarating adventures. A writer of great verve and energy, with a deliciously rich and complex voice, reading Damien is a joy. Take a deep breath before diving in!"

Anna Saunders, founder/CEO Cheltenham Poetry Festival, author of *Communion, Kissing the She Bear, Struck, Burne Jones & the Fox, Ghosting for Beginners* and *Feverfew.*